THE LAST THIRTY
DEVOTIONAL

THE LAST THIRTY DEVOTIONAL

A 30-day Guide to Living your Best Year Before it Begins

BRIA GILMORE

Equip Her Coaching Inc

To the One who created me,
to the One who saved me,
and to the One who empowers me each day,
I give my all to You.

CONTENTS

Introduction

There's a saying that I often heard while growing up in Alabama. "Leave right." My three siblings and I grew up in a family where life lessons and values from our grandparents were taught using simple statements like this one. My grandfather and great grandmother would share stories about growing up during the Jim Crow era, and at the end of every story was a wisdom-filled statement much like "leave right." Savory aromas of baked chicken, collard greens, and candied yams (my favorite) filled the air, a host of loved ones filled the table, and strong values filled our hearts as we simultaneously admired and feared the wisdom gained from their unfathomable experiences.

Many of the lessons from family dinner remain in my heart today, but the one that I often revisit is "leave right." Now, this statement was mostly used in the context of someone exiting a job and starting a new one. If we were accepted to a new job, my siblings and I were always encouraged to end our time in the old place of employment having given our maximum effort through the very last hour on the clock. My takeaway from this saying was that the way I finish one thing will directly impact how I start something else. Considering the same workplace example, if I end my time at a job by giving everyone "a piece of my mind" or by sending an angry email, I might find it difficult to respect a superior or team member in my new role. If I eat terrible food for dinner, I will feel nauseous the next morning. If I decide not to stick to my budget this month, I may find myself struggling to get back on track for next month.

The reality is that the values and habits we maintain in one season will exist in the next. We need much more than a "change of scenery" to truly experience lasting transformation in our character. There is great deception in surmising that the *next* job, the *next* relationship, or the *next* place of living will provide the satisfaction that can only be found in doing the hard work of getting healthy now.

Too many times, we decide that we will wait until January 1 to enact a new purpose or a real change in our lives. It's my hope that as another year's end draws near, we'll live with a purposeful approach *now* rather than attempt to wait for the *next*. Let's be honest, friend. Nothing changes at the stroke of midnight on New Year's Day. We will not wake up and suddenly have better eating habits, relational habits, or work-related habits. We have to make intentional decisions today in order to see lasting change and truly experience a fulfilled life.

It does not matter how we started the year; what matters is how we finish. Over the next 30 days, we'll journey to live more purposefully in five key areas. They are designed to slowly work from the outside (physical and relational) to the inside (spiritual and emotional). There's no better time than now to allow God to lead us to a life truly worth living!

Before You Begin:
- Fully Commit - Throughout this devotional, we'll focus on five key areas of our lives. Even if one area's challenges seem to be easy, do them anyway. There is so much value in remaining committed to something for thirty days.
- Keep a Journal - I encourage keeping a journal throughout this journey to complete daily challenges and to make note of any personal reflections.
- One Day at a Time - Read one devotional a day and complete the challenge. If a day is missed, simply move on to the current day's devotional to stay on track.
- Accountability - I am an avid proponent of inviting people in our lives to help hold us accountable. The Last Thirty challenge is no different. Encourage a trustworthy person to join you.

The last thirty days of the year begin on December 2nd. Of course, this 30-day challenge can be completed at any time. I'm just thrilled to approach the next 30 days with great purpose to set ourselves up for great success in the season to come.

Physical

"Take care of your body. It's the only place you have to live."
- Jim Rohn

Or do you not know that your body is a temple of the Holy
Spirit within you, whom you have from God?
- 1 Corinthians 6:19 ESV

The physical body is the temple of the Holy Spirit. It is the place we've been given to steward. If given the right to lead, our bodies will take us down a path towards unhealthy patterns guided by impulsive cravings. Over the next 6 days, we will consider some of our physical habits. Each day, let's ask the Holy Spirit to reveal where He might want us to pay closer attention as we steward His dwelling place.

Day One

And Nehemiah, who was the governor, and Ezra the priest and scribe, and the Levites who taught the people said to all the people, "This day is holy to the Lord your God; do not mourn or weep." For all the people wept as they heard the words of the Law. Then he said to them, "Go your way. Eat the fat and drink sweet wine and send portions to anyone who has nothing ready, for this day is holy to our Lord. And do not be grieved, for the joy of the Lord is your strength." So the Levites calmed all the people, saying, "Be quiet, for this day is holy; do not be grieved." And all the people went their way to eat and drink and to send portions and to make great rejoicing, because they had understood the words that were declared to them.

- Nehemiah 8:9-12 ESV

This is the first day of the last thirty days this year. Does this reality stir up grief? Is it discouraging to consider the things that are unaccomplished or incomplete? While navigating through this devotional, we may recognize some areas that cause us to see our shortcomings or our failures. While the natural response is to grieve or feel sad, today, we will follow the instructions of the leaders from Nehemiah 8.

The reading of the scriptures caused the hearts of the people to be grieved as they recognized their own failure to uphold the law. However, the leaders declared it a holy day. Yes, we might have missed the mark all year long, but the fact that we are starting this challenge and setting ourselves up for success is worth celebrating. Zechariah 4:10 NLT says, "The Lord rejoices when the work begins."

May this day be one where we find a new strength from the Lord's delight in our decision. This is a day of rejoicing as we take one step back towards the very reason He created us.

Challenge: As we celebrate, let's think of one **physical** activity that we enjoy and do it. Kick the ball around outside with the kids. Dance around the living room to a fun list of songs. Wives, have sex with your husband. As a day of rejoicing, let's have some fun and not pout.

In your journal, list the Physical Activities you enjoy. Highlight the activity that you will complete today. Below are some ideas.

- Play outside with your kids.
- Crank up the music and have a dance party.
- Learn a trending social media dance and record it.
- For the wives, have sex with your husband.
- Play your favorite sport with a group of friends.
- Attend a dance class.
- Go axe-throwing.

- Head out for some skating (roller or ice).
- Go to a local theme or amusement park.
- Visit a trampoline park.
- Play an active video or VR game.
- Play laser tag.
- Go bowling.

Day Two

Now that same day two of them were going to a village called Emmaus, about seven miles from Jerusalem. They were talking with each other about everything that had happened. As they talked and discussed these things with each other, Jesus himself came up and walked along with them;

- Luke 24:13-15 ESV

About two months ago, my counselor encouraged me to regularly connect with friends who would fill me up rather than deplete me. I had just finished divulging all the details of the semester ahead. Another season of my mentoring program for high school girls would soon be launching. My responsibilities as a staff member at my local church were about to increase. Along with that, I knew that the dream of this very book was on my radar to begin.

So, I decided to reach out to a very new friend, Rachel, who had experience working in ministry as well, and asked her to meet once a week. Our meetings vary from coffee dates, lunch, and, many times now, walks at a local trail. Our time together is always filled with a mixture of laughs and honest conversations, but there is something special about our trail walks. There is a subtle force that causes us to dive below the surface because there are very few distractions. For some unknown reason, it feels easier to share something that is on my heart.

When I consider the stories we read in the Bible, we often see walking was the primary mode of transportation. There might have been some who traveled with chariots, others with animals and carts, but the majority of them walked to their destination. It was during these walks that stories were shared, meaningful lessons were taught, and people in need were encountered. When forced to go slowly and without urgency, you can take in everything that's happening. Many of Jesus' lessons, miracles, and challenges were as He and his disciples were on their way somewhere. Even the journey towards the place he would be crucified was a long, slow walk. Take that in for a moment.

In a hurried society, we will have to fight against the literal rushing current that demands urgency over intentionality. Our culture uses oxymoronic words like "fast-paced" or "speed walk". This is not the point of life, nor is it the point of each day. We should see the people around us, hear the words that are spoken, and be fully present in this blessing of a day. What my trail walks with Rachel offer is an intentional pause from the hurries of life to share stories, disclose struggles, and laugh A LOT.

Challenge: Go for an intentionally slow walk. Take in every part of the experience. Allow all five senses to engage. Find appreciation in all that's taken in. In the urgency of this season and those to come, we have to be skilled at slowing down. Consider more purposeful ways to slow down over the rest of this challenge.

Use your journal to answer these reflection questions.

- What did you observe as you walked? What do you appreciate about what was observed?
- Any smells that greeted you on your walk? What did these smells remind you of?
- Did you stop for anything on your walk? A snack or a hot cup of coffee?
- How did it feel? Was it a cool morning outdoors or a long warm walk through the corridors of a hallway?
- What sounds did you notice? Did any of these sounds evoke any emotions?

Day Three

"Remember the Sabbath day, to keep it holy. Six days you shall labor, and do all your work, but the seventh day is a Sabbath to the Lord your God. On it you shall not do any work, you, or your son, or your daughter, your male servant, or your female servant, or your livestock, or the sojourner who is within your gates. For in six days the Lord made heaven and earth, the sea, and all that is in them, and rested on the seventh day. Therefore the Lord blessed the Sabbath day and made it holy.

- Exodus 20:8-11 ESV

I remember when I first joined staff at my local church in the Spring of 2015. Besides the lead pastor, I was the first part-time hire of a two-year-old church plant. As you can imagine, much of the responsibility of operating the church fell on a small group of people. I struggled with feelings of failure because I had not too long before left my previous job after only working with them for six months. Because of this, I found constant validation from doing a good job with the church. After a few successful weeks on the job, I quickly landed in an unhealthy space of making myself available ALL of the time in order to please everyone else. Thankfully, I had already established the habit of taking one day a week to rest. However, in this new position, I felt pressured to cut into my established rest time for work's sake. It was my own insecurity driving that pressure. It didn't take long for my need for rest to cry out for some attention. I fought the urge to people-please and gathered the necessary courage to set a healthy boundary to guard one day a week to rest from work.

I can't imagine where I would be if the value of Sabbath had not already been instilled. I'm sure I'd be overworked, bitter, and resentful. Is there a particular day that is set apart for rest? This is a day to experience the restorative rest that the Lord wants to give us. We labor and work hard, and we need time to allow Him to fill us up.

We have toiled all week long. Now, let's pause and take our hands away from the plow. This act says to the Lord, "I entrust myself and all that I've done to you." Faithfully building this practice into our lives will cause our hearts to prefer God's blessing on six days of work instead of our limited efforts on all seven.

Challenge: I recently learned of a book called *Sacred Rest*. The author, Dr. Saundra Dalton-Smith, shares ground-breaking insight on the seven types of rest needed to optimize productivity and increase overall happiness. Rest should be restorative, so as tempting as "vegging" on the couch on a day off work might seem, it might serve us better to get out for another slow walk, engage in conversation with family, or turn off our devices for a couple of hours. Take a look at the types of rest listed in the chart.

In your journal, list which types of rest you need to implement today and how.

7 Types of Rest by Dr. Saundra Dalton-Smith

- Sensory Rest: Turn off screens and reduce noise and light.
- Physical Rest: Sleep and/or do restorative activities.
- Creative Rest: Appreciate the beauty of nature and rest from creative thinking.
- Emotional Rest: Take time to feel and express your feelings (e.g. therapy).
- Social Rest: Spend time alone and time with restorative people.
- Spiritual Rest: Cultivate belonging, love, purpose, etc.
- Mental Rest: Slow down and give your brain a break.

Additional Resource:

- *Sacred Rest: Recover Your Life, Renew Your Energy, Restore Your Sanity* by Saundra Dalton-Smith, M.D.

Day Four

So, whether you eat or drink, or whatever you do, do all to the glory of God.

- 1 Corinthians 10:31 ESV

While preparing to work on this devotional, I turned off an alarm set to remind me to get up from the computer, drink some water, and take a break. As ridiculous as it might seem, if I don't have a reminder to do it, I'll get so distracted by the other demands of the day. As embarrassing as it is to admit, I've gotten home at the end of a long work day and realized that I had not stopped to eat or drink all day.

The reality is that the way we steward the body that God has created for each of us is important. Of the many diets and food challenges that I've heard of, not one of them tell you not to drink water. In most cases, they encourage you to start drinking more of it. Jesus says He gives living water (John 4), so as we drink from His light and truth to find nourishment for our spirits, so we must regularly drink water to find nourishment for our bodies.

I believe we can produce even greater quality in our work when we give our bodies what they need to perform at its best. Each day, when we take in food to eat or beverage to drink, we should actively consider how this will aid in glorifying God. We could begin to replace one cup of another beverage with water for the rest of this challenge. Instead of the second cup of coffee, why not a glass of water? Instead of that glass of wine after a long day, try a glass of water, first, to nourish your body. Whatever we do, let it be done to the glory and satisfaction of the Lord and not ourselves.

Challenge: Look up the recommended amount of water you should be consuming each day, then drink that amount today. You may be in the restroom more often than usual, but that's a good thing. Water is refreshing, and we should build the habit of refreshing our bodies appropriately. Use your journal to write down any challenges you faced and some of the immediate effects you noticed.

Additional Thoughts: The amount of water you should consume varies based on many things including environment, life stage, exercise, and more. Consult with your physician regarding the recommended amount of water you should be drinking.

Day Five

But I discipline my body and keep it under control, lest after preaching to others I myself should be disqualified.
- 1 Corinthians 9:27 ESV

Earlier this year, I decided to participate in a strict sugar-free eating routine for 40 days. It was horrible. The cravings, the irritability, the "hanger," and the withdrawals were an absolute nightmare for about the first 17 or 18 days. There were the times when I forgot to prepare meals for the day, and there was not ONE snack in the breakroom that fell within the parameters of this self-inflicted torture...not to mention the 3 or 4 times a day when I had to convince myself why I was doing this, as I often forgot it. I can proudly say that I have successfully endured this challenge twice now. However, the greatest reward wasn't the weight loss or the clearer mental space; it was certainty in knowing that my body didn't win.

The body is as intricate and miraculous as it is demanding and obstinate. When we lack intentional discipline in stewarding our physical bodies, we leave ourselves vulnerable to the many lures of the flesh. As Paul purposed in his heart to do, so we should discipline our bodies and keep them under control.

When the cravings come, we should discipline ourselves to say no. When the temptation to hit snooze and sleep in rises, let's drag ourselves out of bed anyway. When the lustful desires arise, we can run and tell someone who will help hold us accountable. Let's discipline our bodies, friend. Let's not go into another year where our bodies are the ones calling the shots instead of the Holy Spirit who lives inside of us.

Though it may be difficult, we will be grateful not only for making the decision to discipline ourselves but also for the decision to invite a trusted person into the journey along with us.

Challenge: In your journal, write one way you can be more physically disciplined. Then, write one change that you can implement to get better with this. Finally, share these thoughts with your accountability partner.

Additional Thoughts: A person who struggles with eating too many desserts might decide to establish a rule to only enjoy a sweet treat when eating out instead of allowing desserts in his or her home. Or, a person who struggles with knowingly viewing inappropriate content might decide to utilize an accountability software that sends regular reports of the websites and content they visit to trusted family members or friends.

Day Six

Or do you not know that your body is a temple of the Holy Spirit within you, whom you have from God? You are not your own, for you were bought with a price. So glorify God in your body.
- 1 Corinthians 6:19-20 ESV

I'm the girl who works out each week out of discipline rather than enjoyment. I mean, what's fun about a 5:30 am alarm to go run and jump around? Then, I'm sore for days after. Yeah, that's not my idea of fun at all. Here's what I know, though. My body needs regular exercise in order to remain healthy and in shape. It also needs someone like my trainer to push me in ways that I would never push myself. There is no way that my body would be in the physical shape it's in now if she didn't make me do all those squats, burpees, and planks. The decision I make to push my body to accomplish difficult physical tasks is one way that I know I can steward my body and use it for God's glory.

What if, at the end of this life, we stand before the Father in Heaven and are asked to give an account for how we stewarded the bodies we were given? Imagine standing there recounting all the decisions that may bring up feelings of great reward and great regret.

How might we live our lives differently if we lived with the perspective that our bodies are not our own? I believe that each of us has a purpose and a call for living and God wants to use us to bring glory to His name. The question is, are we caring for our bodies in a way that will ensure that we are physically fit to handle "the race marked out for us" (Hebrews 12:1)?

The decisions we make to eat healthy foods, implement regular exercise, and drink reasonable amounts of water are honorable decisions. Yet, my hope is that the driver for these commitments isn't vanity or an attempt to preserve life but rather an opportunity to live a life that brings the greatest levels of honor and glory to our Maker. It's with physically healthy bodies that we are able to do the great work that the Holy Spirit dwelling inside leads us to do.

Challenge: Complete 30 minutes of moderate physical activity. This means you should be working hard enough to raise your heart rate and sometimes even break a sweat.

In your journal, list the moderate physical activities you enjoy. Highlight the activity that you will complete today. Below are some ideas.

- brisk walking
- riding a bike
- dancing
- hiking
- rollerblading

Relational

"Show me your friends and I'll show you your future."
- Unknown

Do not be deceived: "Bad company ruins good morals."
- 1 Corinthians 15:33 ESV

We are now making a shift towards our relationships. Whether it's your family, your friends, your co-workers, or anyone else in your life, we have to intentionally examine our relationships. The people in our lives are significant and directly influence our perspectives. Each day, ask the Holy Spirit to reveal where He might want you to pay better attention as you steward the relationships you have with the people in your life.

Day Seven

Iron sharpens iron, and one man sharpens another.
*   - Proverbs 27:17 ESV*

I just finished listening to a video message from one of my closest friends, Danielle. We met when we were 12 years old and have seen each other through some extremely difficult moments in our lives. She and I live away from each other, but we communicate just about every day. She's going to call me later this afternoon to talk through a difficult work situation. I'll listen, offer wisdom wherever possible, and pray for her. When I hear "friend", she is one of the special people in my life who comes to mind.

I don't know that there is anything more important for us to examine at this time of year than the friendships we have. The habits of our friends are bound to influence our own habits. Oftentimes, out of loyalty and to avoid grief, we allow unhealthy people to remain in our lives when, in fact, we're well aware of the detrimental effects of their closeness.

As the proverb mentions, we should have relationships that sharpen us. What good is it to hold onto the friendships that dull the vibrancy of who we are in Christ? Friendships are the relationships we choose, so let's be purposeful with our choices. Let's be wise about the current season of life and honest about whether or not a person's friendship is beneficial. If there is a current void in purposeful friendships, consider praying for and actively seeking someone who might be in at least one of the following categories.

- They are in a similar season of life (single, married, raising toddlers, etc.),
- they understand your cultural upbringing (successfully enduring or have overcome similar cultural struggles),
- and someone who is in a similar profession as you (work in ministry, authors, entrepreneurs).

Challenge: Pull out your journal! Write the names of the 3-5 closest people to you. What are the things about them that you like? Considering the suggested categories above, how do the people you identified fit into these categories? Is there a category listed above that you would like to have friendship in?

Finally, list some potential ways you might make new friends. Below are some ideas as well.

- Join an interest group. (E.g. book club, hiking group, etc.)
- Attend cultural events to meet new people.
- Join a group at work to meet others. (E.g. Toastmasters)

Day Eight

Plans go wrong for lack of advice; many advisers bring success.
- Proverbs 15:22 NLT

A few months ago, I was deeply struggling with feelings of loneliness and discontentment with being single and almost thirty. I had an appointment with my counselor already scheduled, but I needed someone to talk to immediately. I remembered my beloved "big sister" from my college days who had walked through a similar season as my own. Though a wife and mom of three beautiful girls now, she could relate to and understand my struggle specifically. I scheduled time to talk to her and she encouraged me, shared the reality of her feelings when she was at this place, and prayed for me. I'm still holding on to the wisdom of that phone call and will very soon reach out again for another dose of faith-filled encouragement.

Wise counsel is key to the success of the plans we make. We all have desires and things we long to accomplish. I've had conversations with people who want to launch organizations and businesses, and somehow they are convinced that their start-up will gross a million dollars overnight. In order to build something great, we need to have patience, persistence, and wisdom from advisers.

While this applies in business, this proverb also applies to life in general. If we want to live a life that is fulfilling, we need to have specific people to help us along the way. I encourage three intentional relationships to consider for our lives.

- Mentor - This should be someone who is a few seasons ahead of you and can offer perspective from their past experiences. You should be asking them a lot of questions. This is the "big sister" I mentioned. She could speak exactly to that specific struggle.
- Accountability Partner - This is someone who is in a similar life stage. You should be asking each other questions and offering encouragement as you navigate challenges. I have a friend who is in the same season of life and we encourage each other and hold one another accountable during our weak moments.
- Counselor/Therapist - This is a professional who can assist you with emotional and mental struggles that you may not have the tools and resources to complete on your own. For the times when the emotional burden is too heavy, this person can assist with processing many of the difficult thoughts or feelings.

Let's make the decision to seek out these trusted advisers, today, and the "next year" version of us will be grateful we did.

Challenge: Use your journal to answer the following questions:

- Who are the people in your life that offer wise counsel?
- If you have them, are these people willing to tell you when you might be wrong as well as when you're right?
- If you do not have wise counsel, why do you think this is the case?
- How might you intentionally seek out wise counsel in the form of the areas discussed above?

Day Nine

Be kind to one another, tenderhearted, forgiving one another,
as God in Christ forgave you.

- Ephesians 4:32 ESV

Last week, I received an unexpected voice message from an old friend. In this voice message was an apology that I never saw coming. He mentioned that the Lord brought me to mind and thought it necessary to reach out and apologize for something from almost ten years ago. This friend's message fostered deeper respect for him as he reached out to do this. Though I had worked through much of the forgiveness that was necessary for me to move on in life, I realize that many people don't have the same story to tell.

I've heard it said, "Unforgiveness is like drinking poison and expecting the other person to die." Though harsh, this statement is filled with valuable truth. When we decide to withhold forgiveness from those who have wounded or hurt us in the past, we set up barriers for ourselves to make healthy progress. Please understand, forgiveness is a process, and some cases require professional assistance. However, the best thing that you decide to do might be to begin the journey.

Choosing to forgive leads us to offer someone else the greatest gift that we've received from God through Jesus Christ. Forgiven people forgive people. We should be spurred on to embark upon the journey of forgiveness with others because of the way "God in Christ forgave." Let's choose not to allow another year to come without having actively taken steps to process the wounds and hurts from the people who are closest to us.

Challenge: Journal your answers to these questions.

- Are there any offenses or hurts from your past that evoke emotions as if it happened recently?
- Do you have any anger, resentment, or bitterness towards a particular person?
- Have you decided that you'll only extend forgiveness to someone if they prove themselves worthy of it?

Forgiveness is a process that is challenging but certainly worth taking. The forgiveness journey has much less to do with the offender as it does with you and your ability to healthily move forward. My advice is to get assistance from a licensed professional who can help you as you heal. I particularly recommend a professional with a Christian perspective to help you through this.

Additional Books & Bible Study Resources:

- *Forgiving What You Can't Forget* by Lysa Terkeurst
- *The Forgiveness Journal* by Lysa Terkeurst
- *The Freedom and Power of Forgiveness* by John MacArthur
- Focus on the Family offers a plethora of resources including forgiveness within marriages, teaching forgiveness to your children, and much more.

Day Ten

You shall treat the stranger who sojourns with you as the native among you, and you shall love him as yourself, for you were strangers in the land of Egypt: I am the Lord your God.
- Leviticus 19:34 ESV

I have the privilege of working from a co-working office space. Instead of all working for the same organization or business, each "co-worker" works for various businesses or is self-employed. Sitting across from me, today, is a fun and talkative art curator. Tomorrow, I could be across from my teammate working on a project. The next day, I could be across from a developer for a tech company. I love it. I get to meet so many new people and it breaks up the monotony of having the same conversations all the time.

There are people who never meet a stranger. No matter the time or place, quickly establishing connections with new people seems to happen with ease. Every day we come into contact with strangers. Though strangers, I don't believe these encounters are random. Will you have eyes to really see the cashier at your grocery store, the person at the drive-thru window, or the teller at your local bank?

What if a purposeful day meant being a blessing to the "strangers" we encounter? May we treat the people who sojourn with us, though for a moment, with love and kindness.

Challenge: Start a conversation with someone you encounter during a routine activity. Choose to purposefully engage. Below are some quick conversation starters to try. If the person refuses to engage with you, that's ok. In your journal, reflect on your experience completing today's challenge. Was it awkward? How did the other person respond?

- Find something to compliment a person on and inquire about it further.
  - Example: Wow, those are such cute shoes. Are they comfortable?
- Learn about the experience of cashiers and other workers in various establishments.
  - Example: What do you enjoy most about working here?
- Ask for their recommendation.
  - Example: Everything on the menu looks delicious. What would you recommend?
- Listen to the story of how they got started in their line of work.
  - Example: How did you end up working for that nonprofit? Was this something you've always been interested in?

- For someone you know a little, mention something that will give you an update about them.
    - Example: I heard that you recently launched a podcast. How has that experience been for you?

Day Eleven

Above all, keep loving one another earnestly, since love covers a multitude of sins. Show hospitality to one another without grumbling. As each has received a gift, use it to serve one another, as good stewards of God's varied grace.

- 1 Peter 4:8-10 ESV

This past weekend, I had the chance to take some time off work for what I called a "Rest Retreat". One of my teammates and dear friends, Tiffany, had been hearing about this retreat of mine for weeks. She knew all of the details as well as some of the things I decided not to do because of costs. Well, on the first day of my retreat, I got a text from her that she was stopping by to give me something. When she arrived, I opened the door and she had put together an entire Rest Retreat basket. Inside of this basket was a cozy sweater that I unapologetically admit to wearing most of the retreat weekend, a journal (which is a tell-tale sign of knowing me well), some other goodies, and a gift card for a facial at my favorite local spa. She couldn't have loved me any better than that.

Serving one another is a countercultural thought considering that we live in a society that glorifies convenience and self-gratification. To build a life that is built on inconveniencing ourselves will be challenging, but it is necessary to live intentionally. To use our gifts and skills to serve someone else instead of ourselves is to live as a good steward of God's grace.

If we are gifted in speaking, then our words should build up our loved ones instead of criticizing them. If we are gifted with faith, then our prayers should be in full faith for those in our lives who need a miracle and need to experience the hope of Christ.

Challenge: Serve One Another. Do a selfless act of kindness for someone close to you. Remember that not everyone will know how to respond to kindness. How the person responds does not matter, what matters is that you used your resources to serve someone else. In your journal, share about your experience completing today's challenge. Was it difficult? How did the receiving person respond?

Selfless Acts of Kindness for Loved Ones

- Actively listen to what a friend of your has going on and do something special for it. (For example, Tiffany and the rest retreat basket of goodies I shared about.)
- Send someone their favorite flowers.
- Send a voice recording of a prayer or a song (if you sing well) to a friend having a rough day.
- Wake up in time to make a cup of coffee for your spouse before their day.

- Write a note to your child reminding them that you love them and are proud of them no matter what.
- Take off of work a little early to help out a friend working on a house project.
- Text your sibling an old photo of the two of you along with a note sharing that you love them, respect them, and are proud of them.
- Call a parent or another special relative just to ask them about their day.

Day Twelve

So then let us pursue what makes for peace and for mutual up-building.

- Romans 14:19 ESV

On Day 9, I shared about a friend from years ago who sent me an apology. What I didn't share was that for many years, I had wanted to offer an apology of my own, but I had never found the courage to do it. His decision to be obedient fostered an immediate opportunity to communicate my own imperfections and finally ask for forgiveness. Pride had a funny way of creeping in and helping me justify why I shouldn't reach out, but I thank God for his grace through this life journey of imperfection as well as that friend's decision to choose humility.

Today, let's be encouraged to set our sights on humility and asking for forgiveness. As much as we'd like to think it, we are not perfect. In the same way that others wound us, we unintentionally (or, intentionally) hurt others. What a refreshing feeling it will be as we walk into this next year having confessed our mistakes and asked for forgiveness.

Whether or not the other person decides to forgive is irrelevant. It's the intentional decision to humble ourselves that strengthens our resistance to pride. Humility is key in this challenge. We should be willing to examine our hearts and ask for wisdom to see where we need to ask forgiveness from God or someone else or both.

Challenge: Use your journal to answer the following questions:

- Is there someone you need to offer an apology to?
- What do you specifically need to apologize for?
- Is there something from long in the past that needs to be considered?

If at all possible, apologize. Initiate a call or sit down to a face-to-face conversation and apologize. Note: Everyone has a different apology language. Review the Additional Resources to access the apology languages.

Additional Resources:

- *When Sorry Isn't Enough: Making Things Right With Those You Love* by Dr. Gary Chapman and Dr. Jennifer Thomas
- Take the Apology Language Quiz - https://www.5lovelanguages.com/quizzes/apology-language

Soul: Mental & Emotional

"Your emotional health won't change how God shows up for you, but it might change how you show up for Him."
- Dr. Anita Phillips

A joyful heart is good medicine, but a crushed spirit dries up the bones.
- Proverbs 17:22 ESV

The very essence of our being and life is our soul. It is the place where our mind, will, and emotions live. Emotional and mental health are vital as we quickly approach the year ahead. Many of us tolerate "stinkin' thinkin'" as well as unhealthy emotional behaviors, and this could be the very thing that is hindering us from reaching the heights to which we desire to ascend. Let's take the time to allow the Holy Spirit to speak to us about these areas.

Day Thirteen

Beloved, I pray that all may go well with you and that you may be in good health, as it goes well with your soul.

- 3 John 1:2 ESV

On Day 11, I shared about my "Rest Retreat". This three-day retreat included a combination of meaningful conversations with friends and much-needed soul care in solitude. I had planned some time to try a new recipe for flourless pumpkin bread. I quickly admit that the experience was not restful at all. Though I enjoy baking, this activity required more exertion than the rest or enjoyment that it provided. However, later that day, I decluttered my closet. Now, that provided me with a very rewarding and enjoyable feeling. Though the weekend was experimental in a way, I have a deeper appreciation for the time I make to care for my soul.

The writer in 3 John exclaims that he prays that the readers' physical health would be in the same manner of wellness as their soul. The question arises, *how well is it going with our souls?* We all have jobs, people, and responsibilities that require our energy, our emotions, our decisions, and the life from our very being. If all we do is pour and pour into these things, we will eventually find ourselves empty and dry.

We have to do a better job with prioritizing caring so that we can be refilled and refreshed. I pray, as the writer explained, that our souls are well so that our health and physical bodies might be well, too. May this upcoming year be filled with more intentional times where we decide to care for our souls.

This is the perspective I have as it relates to soul care. Jesus is the giver of rest, yet He uses various channels through which His rest flows to us. My trust and hope is not in the weekly pedicure or girls' night out. Matthew 11:28-30 reminds us that when we come to Jesus, we will find all the rest, care, and respite that our soul needs. Make space for soul care activities, but let's remember that Jesus is the One giving our souls the rest they need so we put our trust in Him, not the activity itself.

Challenge: Think of one soul care activity that refreshes you. Do it! Set the time this week to make it happen if you can't do it today. For those who have never taken time for themselves, you might feel uncomfortable or even guilty, but I challenge you to make this a regular practice.

In your journal, list the self care activities you enjoy. Highlight the activity that you will complete today. Below are some ideas.

- Detox bath
- Face mask
- Pedicure (DIY or at a salon)
- Light a candle
- Journal
- Take a slow walk
- Spa day
- Dress up and go out
- Spend time with non-draining people
- Do something nice for someone (Believe it or not, this can be helpful.)
- Watch the sunrise or sunset.
- Get some exercise
- Declutter a space or room in your home.

Day Fourteen

All the days of the afflicted are evil, but the cheerful of heart has a continual feast.

- Proverbs 15:15 ESV

I occasionally have discouraging days, and if I'm not careful I let the defeating feelings shape my perspective and outlook on my life. My opinions become more pessimistic and my countenance turns more melancholic. Now, for anyone who knows me at all, they know this is quite unusual behavior for me. One day when I was feeling pretty down after work, I turned on Katy Perry's "Smile." Not only does the music ignite an instant joy and desire to sing out loud, the words are relatable, too. Needless to say, I danced and sang my entire drive and was uplifted by the time I arrived home.

Hard days will come. That is one of the few guarantees in life that can be made. If we're not in the middle of difficulty, we're either just overcoming it or we might be walking into it. No matter the harshness of this reality, we can purposefully set habits to anchor us in the face of tragic storms in life.

This word of wisdom from Proverbs 15:15 explains that two types of people go through difficult days: the afflicted and the cheerful of heart. They both are walking through painful seasons and moments, but there is something that distinguishes the way they get through these times. The days of the afflicted, downcast heart are evil. They result in depression, seeking pleasure in temporary things, and despair. Yet, the person with a cheerful heart has a continual feast.

Will we choose to feast on God's word, gratitude, and the very fact that we are alive? Our perspective is everything, and there are times when we have to reignite gladness in our hearts. If not now, we can be prepared for the future day that we'll need it.

Challenge: Create a music playlist of 15-20 songs that give rise to joy and lift your spirits. When you have a down day, there's something already available to help bring you up again.

Use your journal to list some uplifting songs you enjoy. Below are some from my Happy Playlist. Choose songs that uplift you, no matter how cheesy or what others think, it's your list.

- "Smile" - Katy Perry
- "(I Want to Say) Thank You" - Orange Kids Music
- "I Like Me" - Kirk Franklin feat. Da' T.R.U.T.H.
- "Masterpiece" - KB
- "Not Today Remix" - Hillsong UNITED
- "Won't Let Go" - Travis Greene
- "No Matter (Basic Tape vs. Frances)" - Basic Tape
- "Look Up Child" - Lauren Daigle
- "Better When I'm Dancin'" - Meghan Trainor

Day Fifteen

Oil and perfume make the heart glad; So does the sweetness of a friend's counsel that comes from the heart.
- Proverbs 27:9 AMP

"I've been really struggling with something." An amazing couple who I love dearly sat across the dinner table and responded, "Oh yeah, what's going on?" Holding back emotions, I proceeded to share how I had been struggling with a decision that had the opportunity to impact my life in a pretty significant way. Fully aware of my own struggle with pleasing people, I needed someone who loved and knew me deeply to give counsel. Sure enough, the husband gave the most poignant piece of advice. I held back tears so grateful to have a place where I could wrestle through emotions and decisions and have such great counsel.

In the relationship section, we talked about the importance of healthy friendships because of the healthy influence that results from them. As it relates to our emotional health, we will need to lean on our friendships for the soul benefits. Soul benefits include deep satisfaction from being fully known. These benefits can only be experienced in our connections with those we expose our vulnerabilities and secrets to. If we meet regularly with those we have called friends yet withhold from them our deepest struggles, we will never experience the fullness to which our friendships were designed for and our souls desperately long for. In his book, *The Common Rule: Habits of Purpose for an Age of Distraction*, Justin Whitmel Earley beautifully shares:

> *The question "Is there anything you aren't telling me?" gets at the heart of friendship, because friendship is being known by someone else and loved anyway. Friendships in which we're vulnerable make or break our lives. With them we thrive, and without them an essential part of us—if not all of us—dies.*

The couple I mentioned knows and loves me well, but I still had to work extremely hard to expose my humanity. As awkward as it might be the first few times, we have to be willing to shine light on the hidden things with the important people in our lives. When we engage in conversation, share our struggles, and encourage one another, we will find healing and restoration for our souls. As we reflect, consider the 3-5 closest people identified on Day 7. Do these relationships offer the deep level of vulnerability that leads to a life that thrives?

Challenge: Establish a weekly face-to-face connection with a friend. This could be over coffee, at the park while your kids play, or after the kids fall asleep and you can sit on the front porch. You could establish this with a friend who might be long distance, but I recommend blocking out time for a face-to-face video call during an uninterrupted time. In your journal, write down who you would like to initiate these deep conversations with and why.

You should both be answering and asking questions similar to these below.

- "Are there any blind spots that I might be unaware of?" Share any red flags that might be of concern. Welcome any feedback without taking offense. You've selected this friend to be in your life because you know they love you and desire what's best for you.
- "Is there anything that you aren't telling me?" Share any secrets or struggles that you're dealing with in any area of your life. Listen to one another and offer support by helping one another determine the best next step towards healing. No matter how embarrassing or painful, be willing to bring light to any darkness.
- "Is there anything I can be praying for this week?" Pray for one another before you leave your conversation and until you meet again.

Additional Resource:
The Common Rule: Habits of Purpose for an Age of Distraction by Justin Whitmel Earley

Day Sixteen

Give thanks in all circumstances; for this is the will of God in Christ Jesus for you.
- 1 Thessalonians 5:18 ESV

In the Fall of 2015, I walked into a grief support group for the very first time. I had lost my older brother and my grandfather within a six month time period that year, and I knew I needed to walk through the journey of grief. We were asked to keep a journal during that semester. The group leader advised writing down anything we felt, memories that came to mind, or things we were grateful for regarding our loved ones. Each week, we'd meet and discuss a topic within the context of navigating grief, but during the week I'd write down reasons I was grateful for those family members in my life. Whenever I wrote down memories of my brother or grandfather, I would always end my writing with gratitude for the impact they had made and that I had the privilege to know them. It was the only time in my life, so far, that I tangibly experienced the transformative power of gratitude in difficult circumstances. I thought the idea of a gratitude journal was bogus until this exercise of writing in my grief journal led me to find reasons to be thankful for the loved ones I had unexpectedly lost.

There are endless studies on the positive physical, relational, and emotional effects of gratitude on those who are depressed. Science confirmed what the Bible has been teaching us all along. God taught his chosen people to bring "thank offerings" to the temple to sacrifice. He created the Passover feast to remember what the Lord did for the people of Israel in Egypt. The significance of remembering and giving thanks is encouraged and even commanded over and over again.

This letter to the church of Thessalonica is no different. The writer explains to give thanks in ALL circumstances. Gratitude is one of the most powerful tools that will keep our perspectives, our hearts, and our lives at their best amidst the most challenging times.

Challenge: In your journal, write out a gratitude list. Simply record the things that you are grateful for today. Write down something different tomorrow. If you take nothing else away from this challenge, I hope that you build this into your life daily. Gratitude is healing to the soul.

Additional Resource:

"What is Gratitude and Why Is It So Important?" by Courtney E. Ackerman, MA

Day Seventeen

Where there is no guidance, a people falls, but in an abundance of counselors there is safety.

- Proverbs 11:14 ESV

In 2017, I was plagued by irrationally fearful thoughts about an ex-boyfriend. I developed an unhealthy savior-complex thinking that if I wasn't in his life he'd fail. I thought that I was the only good thing keeping him on the "right track". After breaking up, I experienced debilitating fears which turned into obsessive behaviors wanting to know how he was doing and if he was ok. The thoughts had gotten so bad that I knew that I needed to speak with a professional about them. I was afraid of the false images that were coming to mind.

After meeting with my counselor that August for the first time, I went on a long journey of healing from what I now know as "codependency". What was interesting about the experience was though I went in with one issue, it took years to dig into the layers of childhood trauma and unhealthy perceptions that were driving my behaviors. Now, many years later, I still meet with this same counselor. I joke with her that she knows more about me than anyone else in the world. I don't know what I would do without having someone to professionally counsel me. Today, I emphasize professionals because they are trained to identify things that our friends or mentors might not have the ability to recognize or treat.

Life throws hard blows, and we're all carrying wounds. It is quite helpful to see someone who can help us identify and work through those issues. Even if things may be "ok," there's nothing wrong with going in for a "check up" as one would go to a primary care doctor. Let's not wait until something is wrong. We should do what it takes to invest in and care for our souls well. This will significantly impact our next year.

Challenge: Schedule your first or next appointment with a mental health therapist or psychologist. I have some personal notes regarding my experience with finding my mental health counselor as well as other notes to consider. In your journal, write down any hesitations you might have in this challenge. Also, consider the points below and use your journal to make any notes.

- Preferences - It was my personal preference to connect with a therapist who is a follower of Christ and uses biblical truth as the foundation for their counsel. I also preferred seeing a female as I felt she would be more relatable. These were my only preferences. I recommend determining your negotiable and non-negotiable preferences. Based upon insurance and budget, you might find that not every preference will be met, but determine what's most important to you and start there.

- Specialists - There are licensed mental health professionals who might hold particular training certifications for special treatments to assist with mental health disorders, personality disorders, etc. Occasionally, a therapist might help you identify a past trauma or issue but recommends you seeing a specialist to help you heal through it using a particular method they may not be trained in.
- Costs - There are costs associated with mental health counseling. You can go through your health insurance or pay out of pocket. I decided to budget for monthly out of pocket fees, but I recognize that not everyone will be able to afford this. Contact your insurance provider to understand what is covered under your health insurance. You might also find local resources that are free or low cost by searching for them in your local area.

Additional Resources:

- BetterHelp
- Psychology Today
- Dr. Anita Phillips

Day Eighteen

There is nothing better for a person than that he should eat and drink and find enjoyment in his toil.

- Ecclesiastes 2:24a ESV

Last year, just after Thanksgiving, I invited four of my closest friends to join me at a restaurant to celebrate all of the goals that I had reached that year. We got all dressed up and enjoyed a girls' night with laughter, fun, and chocolate cake, of course. It fit with the season of Thanksgiving, as this was an opportunity to celebrate what was accomplished but also to thank the Lord for providing me with the resources, skills, and abilities to learn and succeed. After that night, I decided to personally institute this as an annual celebration. Just yesterday, I was thinking about how I'd like to celebrate this year and what I'd like to wear. It felt uncomfortable celebrating myself, but I had worked way too hard not to do it.

When's the last time you had fun? How about the last time you laughed? It's quite tempting to allow work, regimen, and business to steal from us the enjoyment of all the hours we've toiled and labored. What good is it to devote hours upon hours of our lives to work yet never enjoy ourselves?

I reflect back, now, to when I started getting accountability with my budget. I struggled with this. There wasn't one line item for me to enjoy. I just saved for my emergency fund, paid the bills, and purchased the groceries. I was challenged to add something for myself. Even if it was only $10 that month, I went and spent that $10 on something I would personally enjoy. What is the point of me working so hard to earn this money but never actually enjoy it?

Many convince themselves that they'll take a vacation after the promotion or take that extra day off after the project ends. We continually prolong the enjoyment of the fruit of our labor. While this doesn't excuse us to be poor stewards of what we have, it does mean we can have fun with our time. Let's intentionally give room to moments of enjoyment and celebration.

Challenge: Intentionally make time to have some fun. Determine an amount for yourself and treat yourself. Whether you can afford to spend $5, $50, or $500, do something regularly to treat yourself and enjoy the fruits of your labor.

In your journal, list what you can do to have fun along with your budget. Below are some ideas as well. Also, journal any thoughts you might have about treating yourself.

- Buy yourself one nice thing or several small things. Determine the budget, first.
- Go see a new movie. You could find a dollar movie or matinee time.

- Go out to eat. Enjoy dinner at home then go out for desserts if the budget is smaller.
- Get outside for a fun outing. Research some local events in your area.
- Host some friends for a game night. Have everyone bring a game or an appetizer.
- Get pampered. Go get a pedicure or buy a new nail polish to use for a DIY pedicure.
- Get creative. Enjoy a night out painting or visit your local craft store for DIY crafts.
- Learn something new. Try a cooking class or find a new recipe online to try at home.

Spiritual

It is the Spirit who gives life; the flesh is no help at all. The words that I have spoken to you are spirit and life.
- John 6:63 ESV

How few of the Lord's people have practically recognized the truth that Christ is either Lord of all or He is not Lord at all!
- Hudson Taylor

Over the past 18 days we've gradually worked our way inwards. We began this journey with our focus on the physical, then we shifted to our relationships, and finally on to our souls (emotional/mental). Though these are areas we can live intentionally and healthily, I believe that true health, joy, peace, purpose, refreshment, friendship, and all that we'll ever need has been lavishly supplied to us from God through Jesus Christ. If we are not anchored in our hope of Jesus Christ, then everything we've learned the past three weeks will be a temporary fix. Is everything on the outside fine, but internally there's still a nagging void? This just might be the area to focus on in order to live more purposefully as we move into the new year. Don't wait. End this year well. "Leave right."

Day Nineteen

For whatever was written in former days was written for our instruction, that through endurance and through the encouragement of the Scriptures we might have hope.

- Romans 15:4 ESV

I have to admit that I often find it easy to implement disciplines into my life. Someone I had dinner with recently said to me, "Bria, you are not normal. You are leaps and bounds ahead of most people your age and older." There is a part of me that feels misunderstood when I hear comments like this. My relationship with the Lord isn't perfect. I skip days of reading my Bible, I wrestle with pride, and I have definitely allowed lust of the flesh to win in moments. However, my relationship with Him is passionate. Most often, people mistake passion for perfection. I hope to never discourage anyone from the incredible gift of remaining faithful to God just because their experience doesn't look like mine. My heart as we walk through this section isn't to convince anyone to be me. However, I will unapologetically admonish every reader to pursue passionate faithfulness to their relationship with the Lord. As a result of a passionate walk with Jesus, we implement disciplines in our lives that will ultimately anchor us during the difficult times that inevitably arise.

The trials and struggles in our lives can be like waves. They crash up against our ships as we sail the seas of life. They rock us and often cause us to drift back and forth. However, the Word of God is a lot like the sea anchor for our lives. There are times when a boat at sea needs to drift, but it can't be completely unmoored. A sea anchor is used to keep a boat pointed in the right direction, particularly when the seas are rough and the waves might be problematic. Life will come with its heavy winds and waves, that's a guarantee, but a devoted passion to the Word will help us endure the storms and keep us encouraged when strong winds try to cause us to drift. Let's establish the Word of God as our anchor before the new year arrives, so that when difficulties emerge, we're held in place.

Challenge: Prioritize the regular readings of God's Word to allow it to become the anchor that gives you strength to endure and encourages you in your faith when you desire to give up. Use your journal as you begin to implement this challenge. This could become your spiritual journal once the thirty days are over. Consider these steps to help you get started.

- Start by reading one chapter a day from one of the Gospels (Matthew, Mark, Luke, and John)

- At the end of your reading, journal answers to these questions
    - What do you notice from the reading? What was said? Who was speaking? Who was the audience? Any other things you noticed?
    - Which parts of the passage stood out to you?
    - Is there anything you might be able to apply to your life or ponder throughout your day?
- Establish a rule that you won't check emails, social media, or the news until you've read through scripture.

Additional Resource:

Swords Up: An Introduction to Using the Bible 21- Day Virtual Course by Bria Gilmore

Day Twenty

Oh how I love your law! It is my meditation all the day. Your commandment makes me wiser than my enemies, for it is ever with me. I have more understanding than all my teachers, for your testimonies are my meditation. I understand more than the aged, for I keep your precepts.

- Psalm 119:97-100 ESV

I can vividly remember a particular session with my counselor about two years ago now. I had been sharing for 20 minutes about a struggle I was having with making a relationship decision. With such strong people-pleasing tendencies, I often struggle with making big decisions because I can sometimes become paralyzed by the fear of failing or letting people down. She walked through the usual process of helping me identify that neither decision is bad and that I could do either thing without worry of sinning or destroying my life.

Then, she asked me, "What does God think about each of these things?" I had to pause because I had been exerting a lot of mental energy for weeks on this decision. I said I was "praying about it" but I had not truly asked God about His thoughts on any of it. She encouraged me to take some time to read verses about relationships and to consider my current decision through the lens of God's Word. Well, it was actually in the middle of my one-year Bible reading plan that the Holy Spirit spoke to me about this very situation from a passage in Deuteronomy. The Lord speaks to us through His Word and offers wisdom and counsel.

In a society that highly values experts, theologians, and gurus, we often find ourselves seeking the knowledge and expertise of human beings. How often do we run to find a book, listen to a podcast, or anything in order to learn more about a particular topic? While these resources might add value, it is the Word of God and the power of His Holy Spirit that will offer greater wisdom and understanding than either of these ever could.

When we find ourselves going through a difficult situation, we must remember the necessity of relying on the Word as that anchoring source. He will speak to us when we are afraid, anxious, lacking joy, and alone. May our default place when seeking wisdom and understanding be at the Lord's table as we feast on the daily bread of His Word.

Challenge: Find a verse that is helpful for something you're walking through right now. Commit it to memory and meditate on it throughout the day. You can use your search engine and find "Bible verses for..." and add a topic. Some might include fear of the future, dealing with a breakup, death of a loved one, forgiving someone, leading a team, or how to handle money. Use your journal to write out the verse(s) you find.

Additional Resource:

- Youversion Bible App is an interactive tool you can use to search scriptures and Bible reading plans based on topics.

Day Twenty-one

And rising very early in the morning, while it was still dark, he departed and went out to a desolate place, and there he prayed.
                                                                - Mark 1:35 ESV

"Good Morning, Daddy." These are usually some of the first words that come out of my mouth when I roll over from a night's sleep. That's my first prayer each day. As I mentioned on Day 19, my relationship with the Lord is quite passionate, which has led to deeper levels of intimacy with Him. I just picture the relationship of an earthly father with his daughter. She might call him "daddy" or another endearment due to the intimacy of their relationship while still revering his role with great honor and respect as the leader and head of her life. That's how I relate to God. It is my relationship *with* Him that sets the tone for the way I relate *to* Him.

Prayer is one of the most beneficial things for everyday life. When we begin to build a life that values the importance of prayer, we'll experience a year significantly different from those in the past. Though prayer can seem intimidating, Jesus modeled prayer in a way that we can practically implement into our lives. Oftentimes, it's easier to let someone else handle prayer, so we ask the person who is "stronger" in their faith to pray for us.

However, it's in the empty places that true intimacy with the Father is formed. Is your time with the Lord only communal? There is great value in gathering with others, but Jesus made it clear that we also have to intentionally get away from everyone else so that we can connect intimately with our Creator. It's in these places that we find refreshment, we find deep connection, and we are reminded that we are not alone.

He loves you and can be trusted. He's not looking for perfect, "Christianese" words; He simply longs for our sincere hearts. Our future selves will truly thank us for making this a focus the last thirty days of the year.

Challenge: Get alone and pray. To help, use your journal to write down your prayer. What would you talk to Him about if He were right there with you? Because He IS there. (Please note that all the days of this section are designed to help you as you grow in your *relationship* with the Lord. The deeper and more intimate that relationship becomes, the easier it might be to talk to Him.)

Additional Resource:

- Pray First App is an interactive tool you can use to learn how to pray.

Day Twenty-two

And let us consider how to stir up one another to love and good works, not neglecting to meet together, as is the habit of some, but encouraging one another, and all the more as you see the Day drawing near.

- Hebrews 10:24-25 ESV

The year was 2020. The greatest threat to our very existence was forcing its way into our lives and homes. Its name? Isolation. I was forced to stay away from the people I encountered every day and stay home. During a season where I thought it might be easier to have phone calls with friends, learn my neighbors' names, and actually have meaningful conversations inside the household, I didn't. At times, I feared that we'd lost the ability to actually socialize due to the effects of significantly increased time on social media. How ironic? Working on staff for a church, I had an up-close view on this heartbreaking reality. I watched families and friendships rip apart because of views and opinions aired out on social profiles. I watched "believers" completely fall away from the faith because of their disappointment with other followers of Christ's behaviors or their disagreement with church leaders because of the way they handled their platforms to speak out for justice.

Distance was great for physical reasons but quite detrimental to one of the greatest human needs of them all - relationships. It's when we get close to one another that we learn how to have healthy conversation and conflict. We were not created and designed to do life alone. When it comes to strengthening our faith in Christ and living devoted to loving each other well, we must recognize the importance of prioritizing our intimate connection with members of the body of Christ. Intimate connection means meeting regularly with fellow believers to be vulnerable, wrestle with living as Christians (even if you don't agree on everything), and caring for one another in times of need.

Please don't fall victim to the illusion that we can change and grow on our own. Community is vital to our spiritual endurance as well as to our fulfillment of our role in Jesus' teachings. Take the time to find a local part of the body of Christ that is life-giving, loving, and disciples you in your unique gifts and talents in order to spread the good news of Jesus.

Challenge: Find a local small group of believers to regularly fellowship with. I recently joined a group of young adult women for the first time. I knew no one, but I showed up anyway. For those who are already plugged into a group, I challenge you to intentionally consider how to stir up one another towards love and good works. You might write encouraging note cards, ask the group how you can pray for them, or send a small gift.

Journal your thoughts about today's devotional and challenge. Are there any hesitations, or do you find this easy to do?

Additional Thoughts: Many local churches offer seasonal small groups. You can search for local church small groups in your area.

Day Twenty-three

For a day in your courts is better than a thousand elsewhere. I would rather be a doorkeeper in the house of my God than dwell in the tents of wickedness.

- Psalm 84:10 ESV

If I'm honest, I vaguely remember a Sunday that I was not at church. My parents rarely fell for my quality acting skills as I attempted to portray a feebly, sick child on Sunday mornings to avoid getting dressed for church. As little kids, we were always in our white stockings, shiny patent leather shoes, and puffy dresses. Ten times out of 10, my twin sister and I were dressed identically to match our already identical faces.

As I reflect on this Sunday morning routine, my parents helped instill the value of going to church. As I write this, I am 29 years old, but I can still quote to you the verses and prayers we were taught in children's church or Sunday school. The point in going to church wasn't meant to result in empty ritualistic behaviors or to put all my trust in a pastor. It was on the foundation of regularly being in that environment that I was able to experience the power of unified faith that cultivated the ground that would eventually make my middle school heart ready to truly accept Jesus. At that point, I was able to fully appreciate the leaders, the community, and ultimately the Word of God.

Considering that the early church had to sneak around in houses and there are movements of the underground church that break the law to gather together to worship, we should delight in the freedom we have to meet together in the name of our Lord, Jesus. Whether it's in a house, a high school, or a sanctuary, let's not give up meeting together as some are in the habit of doing.

It is important for all of us to commit to regularly hearing the teachings of the Word of God by attending a local church. Hebrews 4:12 (ESV) says, "For the word of God is living and active, sharper than any two-edged sword, piercing to the division of soul and of spirit, of joints and of marrow, and discerning the thoughts and intentions of the heart." When we faithfully show up to place ourselves in environments where the teaching of God's word happens, we make ourselves available to the powerful transformation that God wants to do inside of us. It's not the message that transforms us; it's the presence of God. Let's commit to placing ourselves and our families in healthy church environments where the presence of God dwells so that we can all grow and be transformed.

Challenge: Commit to regularly attending church. If you have a church but haven't made it a priority, make plans to attend the next gathering. If you have a church and you do regularly attend, consider who you should invite to join you and do it.

If you've never attended a local church before, it might take some time to find the community that's best for you. Here are a few suggestions for you as you consider what church to regularly attend.

1. Pray First - Ask the Holy Spirit to give you and your family wisdom and discernment as you search for a church home.
2. Ask Someone - If you know someone who is regularly attending church AND their lives are examples of Christ's truth and love, then you might enjoy visiting church with them or getting other suggestions of local churches to visit from them.
3. Active Community Presence - Many churches will host community outreaches and public events which I believe can give you a chance to get to know them. Attend local events or programs hosted by local churches.

Day Twenty-four

Oh come, let us worship and bow down; let us kneel before the Lord, our Maker!

- Psalm 94:6 ESV

Let's read today's scripture, again. Let us worship and bow down. Let us kneel before the Lord. I remember listening to a pastor teach on worship and why it's important in our lives. I would be in a worship service and think about if others were looking at me. If I wasn't comfortable, I would withhold lifting my hands or physically expressing myself in a way that puts various verses of the Bible into practice. The Bible admonishes us to praise with singing, worship with gladness, clap our hands, play instruments, and dance. We were created to worship. During that pastor's teaching, I learned that the act of worship is a simultaneous moment of magnifying the Lord and humbling ourselves.

If we were created to worship, then our very lives should be driving this same theme - worship Him and bow down. When I have a disagreement with a loved one, worship can remind me that He created them and it will cause anger or pride to bow down. If I'm struggling with doubt or fear, I can magnify my Father and who He is, which causes those other things to bow down. When I'm frustrated with people or overwhelmed by my work, I turn on my worship playlist. It reminds me that Jesus is who all this is for, not me, my retirement, or my comfort.

Every aspect of our lives can be the places where worship to the Lord, our Maker, remains. Let's be intentional about entwining worship throughout every part of our journey. Everything I do should be for all of eternity.

Challenge: Start and end your day with songs that magnify the Lord and lead you to bow your life down before Him by creating a Worship Playlist. Below are some from my favorites right now. I'd like to make note that there are many great songs that are biblically sound, but they aren't necessarily the songs I add to this list. Try to select songs that keep you focused on Him. Use your journal to write down the worship songs you enjoy and why.

- "How Great Thou Art - Hymn" (There are various artists who sing this one.)
- "None Like You" - Vertical Worship
- "Agnus Dei/ King of Kings" - Hillsong Worship
- "Alpha & Omega" - Israel & New Breed
- "Over All I Know" - Vertical Worship
- "Wide as the Sky (Live)" - Isabel Davis
- "Worthy of Your Name" - Passion
- "You are God Alone" - William McDowell
- "Jesus, You Alone" - Highlands Worship

Additional Thoughts: You can, also, search "Christian Worship Playlist" on your preferred streaming platform to help you get started.

Dreams & Goals

The plans of the diligent lead surely to abundance, but every-one who is hasty comes only to poverty.
- Proverbs 21:5 ESV

The heart of man plans his way, but the Lord establishes his steps.
- Proverbs 16:9 ESV

Now that we've allowed the Holy Spirit to examine us from the outside in, we will shift to the very area that most people are thinking about right now. Goals help us strategically achieve the desires of our heart. However, in order to set intentional goals, we must create the space to dream purposeful dreams. Goals should be the framework to the blueprints drawn out by our dreams. We're purposefully ending the year creating the space we need to dream big dreams. That way you have a better idea of what you want to set as goals.

Day Twenty-five

For I know the plans I have for you, declares the Lord, plans for welfare and not for evil, to give you a future and a hope.
- Jeremiah 29:11 ESV

For a very short stint, I worked in the corporate finance world. I was fresh out of college, and I had gotten this job working in investments for a large company. I had studied for and passed the required licensing exams then trained for the job's daily tasks. The problem was that after only a couple of months, I realized that I was not at all happy with it. After only six months, I left that job and was completely unsure about what I was supposed to do. As you know, that led to my opportunity to help out at our church. This turned into a part time job on staff. And since then, it evolved into a full time staff position.

What a tragedy it would be to get to the end of this life on earth, whether 5 or 50 years from now, and realize we spent it chasing after something we were never designed to do. I could have easily "stuck it out" in that finance job, but I would have never experienced the fulfillment that has come from doing what

I was made to do. If we embark upon another year just chasing dreams and setting goals that do not align with what God desires most of us, then we'll miss the point of living completely.

The only future and hope that we can bet our lives on is the one God has for us. However, many of us live in the tension of pursuing the things that everyone else pursues while desiring to follow God. The way we clearly discern God's desires for us is by creating the space needed to allow the Holy Spirit to clarify His plans while dimming the view on the plans we have for ourselves.

Challenge: Use your journal to reflect on what your goals were for this year. Whether you accomplished them or not, do you believe that the plans you set out to accomplish were the Lord's plans for you? If yes, why do you think so? If not, why do you think not? Ask the Lord to show you His plans for you and help you as you dream for all that's ahead.

Day Twenty-six

Trust in the Lord with all your heart, and do not lean on your own understanding. In all your ways acknowledge him, and he will make straight your paths.

- Proverbs 3:5-6 ESV

There have been times in my life when I get to the end of the day and realize that I never once considered God. I made all the decisions on my own without ever pausing or praying. I recognize that those are typically the toughest days. I work so hard to see my plans for the day accomplished that I have a hard time making space for God to rework the plans for Himself. Instead of Him being in the driver's seat of my life, I take the wheel and just invite Him to come along for the ride.

I think today is a wonderful opportunity for each of us to reflect on the projects, plans, and goals we've set and ask ourselves if the driver of these plans is Jesus or us. Imagine if we were taking a road trip and realized that we were going the wrong direction. We'd probably stop somewhere, confirm our directions, and then we'd set out going the right way. There is nothing wrong with making a pit stop along the way towards the dreams or goals we have and making sure that we're going in the right direction. This allows us to make sure that we're trusting the Lord to direct us rather than ourselves.

Every time I set out to start a new project, I seek the Lord. I commit the work to Him and ask for the Holy Spirit's wisdom and direction on it. Otherwise, I'll find myself striving and not gaining any traction. To experience straight paths and established plans, we must commit everything we do to Him. Let's approach our work with hands open and hearts surrendered. If we nurture an attitude of acknowledging Him as the driver of our lives and plans, we'll be much better off than most.

Challenge: In your journal, write down the project or plan you have already begun. Would you say that you're the driver of those plans or Jesus? How can you begin to surrender your plans to the Lord? What are the primary motivators for you on this project? Is glorifying the Lord one of those motivators?

Day Twenty-seven

And the Lord answered me: "Write the vision; make it plain on tablets, so he may run who reads it. For still the vision awaits its appointed time; it hastens to the end—it will not lie. If it seems slow, wait for it; it will surely come; it will not delay.
- Habakkuk 2:2-3 ESV

In March of 2018, I was sitting in economy seating of a Virgin Australia airplane crossing the International date line. As my sister slept in her seat next to me and other passengers flipped through tv shows or movies on their screens, I sat with a notebook writing down the first set of plans for what is now the nonprofit organization I founded called EquipHer. My sister and I were headed on an early birthday celebration trip to the top place on my travel bucket list: Australia. It could've been the excitement and adrenaline that wouldn't allow me to sleep, but I had to get all that was swirling in my head down on paper. I still have that notebook with pages of vision for the dream I felt stirring in my heart at the time.

Today, we're going to set aside time to dream. This is our time to dump out all the ideas we have rattling around in our heads. Even though some of these dreams might take a while before we see them come to fruition, we need to write them down. They are a great point of reference for later on down the road when we are in seasons of wandering or just needing clarity. This is a pivotal part of the process that I believe will ignite us as we near the start of a new year.

Challenge: Turn to a fresh page in your journal, because it's time to dream! First, when you get to the end of next year, what would you like to have accomplished? Now, we'll take away the barriers of time. What are some of your wildest dreams? What do you desire to accomplish before the end of your life? Remove any barriers caused by logistics or pessimism.

Day Twenty-eight

And I sent messengers to them, saying, "I am doing a great work and I cannot come down. Why should the work stop while I leave it and come down to you?"

- Nehemiah 6:3 ESV

This Last Thirty devotional has been a labor of love for me. There have been days where I just had to tell people "no" in order to meet self-established deadlines to finish the work. I chose to postpone some appointments and determine the "must do" items on my other work lists to trim down my work load. Sometimes, these are the hardest moments for me. I want to do everything, but like every other human being on the planet, I can't. I had to determine the necessary work that needed my devotion and full attention without allowing the other things to get in the way.

As I consider the quickly-approaching new year, I imagine the many people who abandon their new year goals by February. For most, starting is not the place of difficulty; it's finishing. There's much to learn from Nehemiah as he led a group of people to rebuild the wall of their home city. The verse above is his response to a group of people attempting to stop the work that they were doing. Nehemiah resolved in his heart that the work they were doing was most important.

Are there distractions that come in the form of endless social media scrolling, tv binging, or hanging with people who do not value the work? Will we carry the resolve of Nehemiah to make the work we're doing for the Lord the most important so that we finish? Let's resolve in our hearts to not only be starters but also finishers.

Challenge: In your journal, answer the following questions. What's one thing that you started in the past but didn't complete? Make note of some of the things that hindered your ability to reach this goal. Now, consider your current dreams. What will be directly impacted by the decision not to finish the work? For Nehemiah, it was the future of his home and the generations to come after him. What is it for you?

Day Twenty-nine

The plans of the diligent lead surely to abundance, but everyone who is hasty comes only to poverty.

- Proverbs 21:5 ESV

Last year, I had the dream to launch my first ever virtual coaching course. This was one of those "good idea, wrong timing" ideas. I had developed the content and curriculum and desperately wanted to release it so that I could generate some passive income. Honestly, I was more concerned about the bottom line of my budget rather than planning strategically for this product. I didn't make time to market or intentionally promote it. When the coaching course launched, it did not sell AT ALL. I had invested a lot of energy and time to make it happen, but it was hasty and poorly thought out.

A major hindrance that affects whether or not we achieve our dreams is poor planning. Now that we have our wildest dreams captured on paper, it's time to purposefully take steps towards turning these things into reality. Consider Jesus' words from Luke 14:28-30 (ESV): "For which of you, desiring to build a tower, does not first sit down and count the cost, whether he has enough to complete it? Otherwise, when he has laid a foundation and is not able to finish, all who see it begin to mock him, saying, 'This man began to build and was not able to finish.'"

It's clear that in order to see the work finish, we have to be wise in our planning. We must count the cost of our time, our relationships, our finances, and, most importantly, our skills. We need to take time to see that our plans are executed wisely, so let's do it. Hasty actions can lead to detrimental consequences. For me, it was a lot of lost time, but for others it's much worse. We can be diligent and focused as we make plans and set strategic goals.

Challenge: Review your thoughts from Day 25 to Day 28. Now, let's begin to put some order to the dreams you desire to pursue. Journal your answers to the following questions.

- Define Your Goal
    - What is the dream in your heart?
    - What's a realistic timeline for this goal?
- Identify Your Roadblocks
    - What resources do you need to accomplish the dream in your heart?
    - Are you willing & able to give up something on your schedule to devote the time?
- Critical Elements
    - What specific days/times will you set aside for this dream?
    - What will happen if you don't accomplish this goal?

Day Thirty

Rejoice in the Lord always; again I will say, Rejoice.
- Philippians 4:4 ESV

You did it, friend! It's the last day of Last Thirty. For those who started this challenge on December 2, it should be New Year's Eve! I hope that some of the action steps we covered have sparked some new habits or reignited some old dreams. At the stroke of midnight, nothing magically changes. Yet, because we focused on being purposeful with these last 30 days, we are now on the road towards success.

The challenge is to CELEBRATE. As we read on Day 18 *There is nothing better for a person than that he should eat and drink and find enjoyment in his toil. - Ecclesiastes 2:24a (ESV).* We have to remember to celebrate when we have worked hard to crush the goals we set. You completed this challenge, so celebrate that. And, as you plan, make sure you intentionally plan celebrations along the way.

I couldn't be more proud of you. I believe that this year will be one of the most intentional yet because of what you set in your heart to do these last 30 days. You're leaving this year right. That's what this was all about. So, as you step into another season, consider the habits, relationships, and goals that you'll take with you into the new year as well as those you'll leave behind. Well done, my friend. I pray that this has been as much of a delight for you as it has been for me.

List what you can do to celebrate. Below is that same list of ideas from Day 18 to consider.

- Buy yourself one nice thing or several small things. Determine the budget, first.
- Go see a new movie. You could find a dollar movie or matinee time.
- Go out to eat. Enjoy dinner at home then go out for desserts if the budget is smaller.
- Get outside for a fun outing. Research some local events in your area.
- Host some friends for a game night. Have everyone bring a game or an appetizer.
- Get pampered. Go get a pedicure or buy a new nail polish to use for a DIY pedicure.
- Get creative. Enjoy a night out painting or visit your local craft store for DIY crafts.
- Learn something new. Try a cooking class or find a new recipe online to try at home.

In your journal answer the final questions as you end the Last Thirty challenge.

- Which particular challenge(s) would you like to continue as you begin the new year? Why?
- Which particular points made throughout the last thirty days resonated most with you? Why?
- Which one of the dreams you identified would you be most proud of yourself for prioritizing?

What Next?

One night, somewhere around 1:00 am, I found myself feeling the same adrenaline I described as I jotted down notes on that plane ride to Australia on Day 27. I had more ideas that I needed to write down. Later that week, I connected with a church member over coffee. I shared all the ideas I had but I also admitted that I felt stuck and wasn't sure where to begin. It was nice dreaming about it all, but I was so overwhelmed by all of it that I didn't feel motivated to do anything. He began to ask me questions, and I started to realize how good he was with logistics and organizing. I didn't really need his help executing on any of the goals or dreams. I needed his unbiased perspective to coach me into organizing my thoughts and holding me accountable to take the next big steps. On occasion, I do still struggle with making those big decisions, so he lovingly corrects and helps me get back on track.

Some of us might read through this and think, "Well, that was great for me." Others might be thinking, "I've got all these ideas, but what should I do now?" For those who resonate most with the latter, I highly recommend investing in a life coach. A good coach of a sports team helps teach the fundamentals of the sport, conditions players for the physical toil ahead, strategizes plays to help them win the game, and monitors along the way to make necessary shifts and changes, all while keeping the team on the road towards winning a championship.

A life coach essentially does the same thing with their clients. As a certified life coach, I teach people the fundamentals of discovering life purpose through Christ, condition them with exercises to set goals, give strategic plays for them to reach their life goals, and assess along the way towards finishing the work they've set out to do. Sometimes, we need an extra pair of eyes helping us strategically approach our goals. If you don't have this, I certainly encourage it.